Excellent!
©Disney/Pixar

Perfect work!
©Disney/Pixar

Yo
©Disney/Pixar

Top effort!
©Disney/Pixar

I love to read!
©Disney/Pixar

Well done!
©Disney/Pixar

Let's have fun!
©Disney/Pixar

Well done!
©Disney/Pixar

You deserve a reward!
©Disney/Pixar

Excellent!
©Disney/Pixar

An awesome effort!
©Disney/Pixar

Good effort!
©Disney/Pixar

Take your time
©Disney/Pixar

Well done!
©Disney/Pixar

Well done!
©Disney/Pixar

Good work!
©Disney/Pixar

I love to read!
©Disney/Pixar

Word perfect!
©Disney/Pixar

Let's have fun!
©Disney/Pixar

Good effort!
©Disney/Pixar

You deserve a reward!
©Disney/Pixar

Top effort!
©Disney/Pixar

Good effort!
©Disney/Pixar

STEPS TO READING

Dear Parent:

Congratulations! Your child is taking the first steps on an exciting journey. **The destination? Independent reading!**

STEPS TO READING will help your child get there. The programme offers three steps to reading success. Each step includes fun stories and colourful art, and the result is a complete literacy programme with something for every child.

Learning to Read, Step by Step!

(1) **Start to Read   Nursery – Preschool**
• **big type and easy words** • **rhyme and rhythm** • **picture clues**
For children who know the alphabet and are eager to begin reading.

(2) **Let's read together   Preschool – Year 1**
• **basic vocabulary** • **short sentences** • **simple stories**
For children who recognise familiar words and sound out new words with help.

(3) **I can read by myself   Years 1-3**
• **engaging characters** • **easy-to-follow plots** • **popular topics**
For children who are ready to read on their own.

STEPS TO READING is designed to give every child a successful reading experience. The year levels are only guides. Children can progress through the steps at their own speed, developing confidence in their reading, no matter what their year.

Remember, a lifetime love of reading starts with a single step!

By Melissa Lagonegro

Illustrated by Art Mawhinney

This edition published by Parragon in 2011

Parragon
Queen Street House
4 Queen Street
Bath BA1 1HE, UK

ISBN 978-1-4454-2106-3

Printed in Malaysia

STEPS TO READING

2

Disney · PIXAR

Cars

Roadwork

PaRRagon

Bath · New York · Singapore · Hong Kong · Cologne · Delhi
Melbourne · Amsterdam · Johannesburg · Auckland · Shenzhen

New cars are coming
to Radiator Springs.
They want to see
Lightning McQueen!

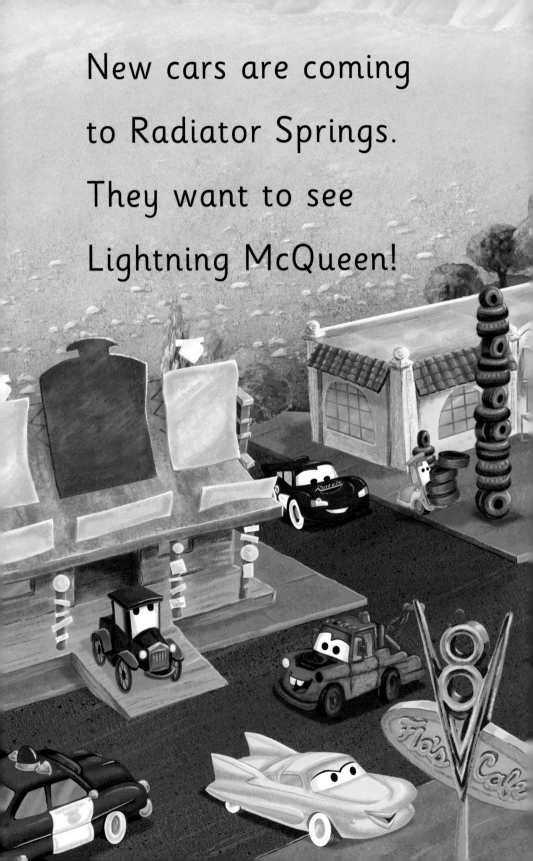

The town is
getting ready.
They have work to do!

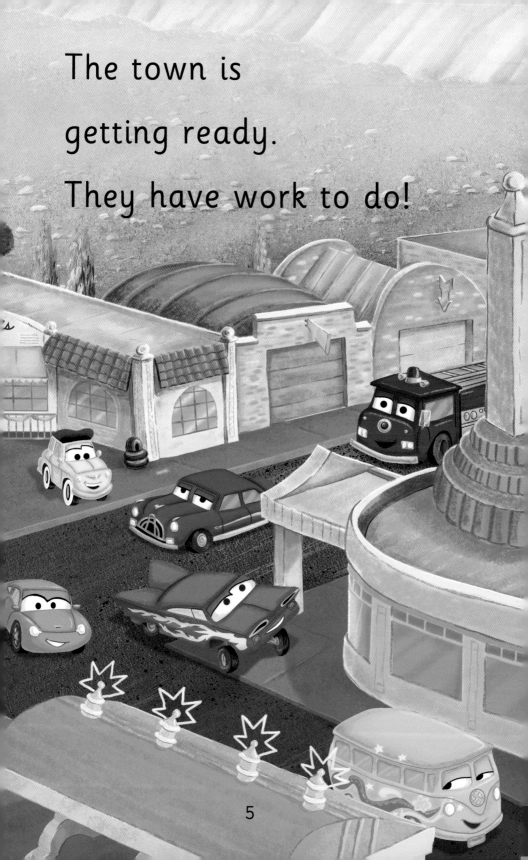

Lightning paves the road.

It will be smooth

for his fans.

Ramone gives himself
a fresh coat of paint.

He is ready to paint
all the new cars
that come to town.

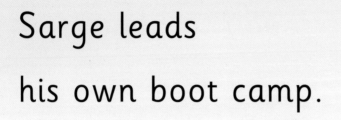

Sarge leads
his own boot camp.

He will get
all the 4x4s that visit
into good shape.

Fillmore makes
his own fuel.
He hopes
Lightning's fans
are thirsty.

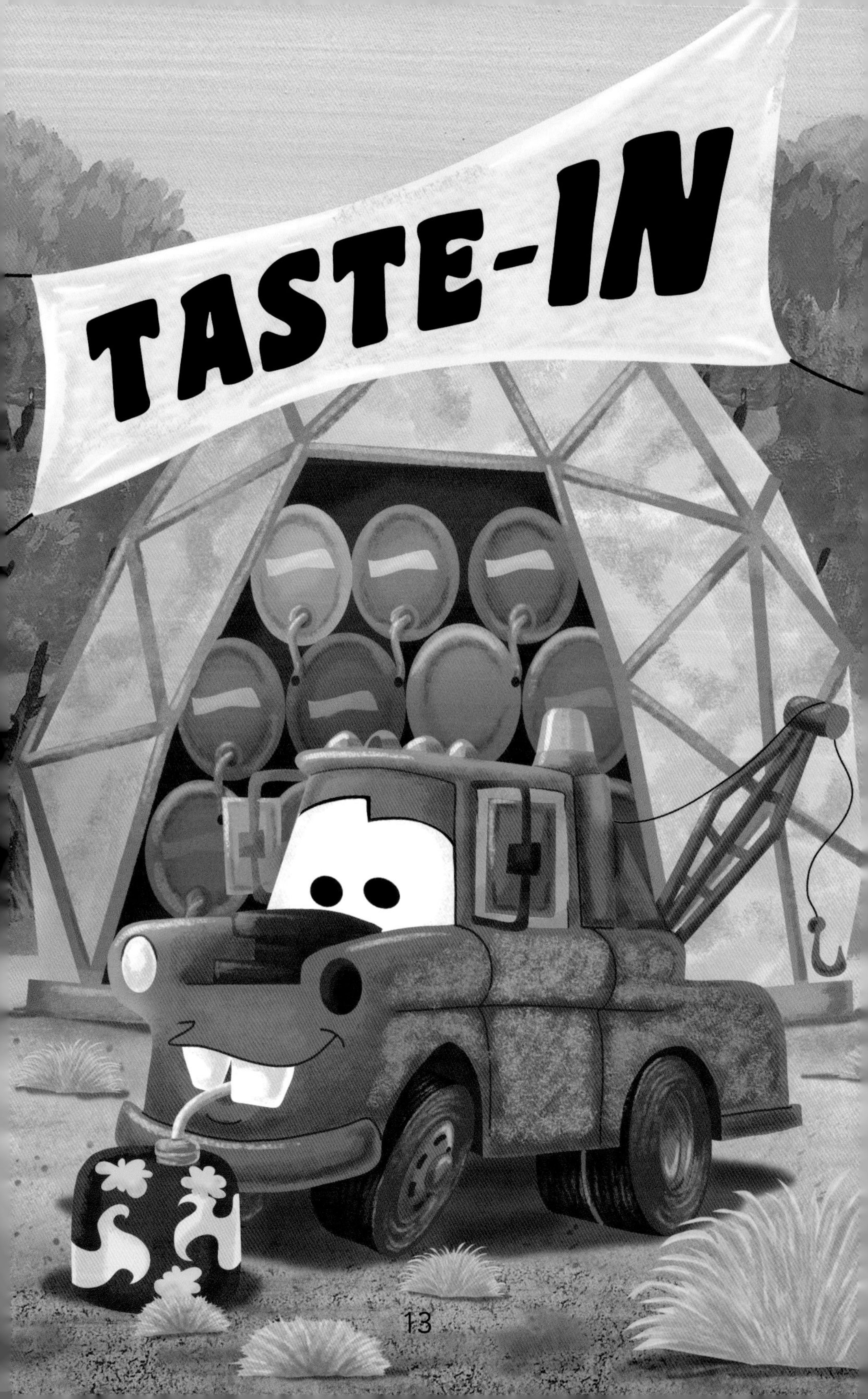
TASTE-IN

At Casa Della Tyres,
Luigi has
new tyres to sell.
Lightning tries them on.

Guido helps, too.
He is a busy forklift.

Flo runs the diner.
Cars visit and sip oil
with friends.

Soon it will be packed
with racing fans.

Red waters the flowers.
He wants the town
to look its best!

Sally fixes up her motel.
It is the perfect place
for guests to rest.

Frank cuts
and harvests grain.
Mater gets Frank to work
extra hard.

Sheriff puts up
new road signs.

He does not want

anyone to speed.

After a long drive,
the cars need a tune-up.
Doc is ready to take
good care of them.

Lizzie gets
new bumper stickers.
She will sell them
in her shop.

Al Oft,

the Lightyear blimp,

flies overhead.

Greetings from

RADIATOR SPRINGS

He lets everyone
in town know
when visitors are
on their way.

29

The town is ready
and the work is done!
The cars go out
and have some fun!

Welcome to

Radiator Springs!

Now turn over for the next story...

Adapted by Apple Jordan

DISNEP · PIXAR

Driving Buddies

PaRRagon

Bath · New York · Singapore · Hong Kong · Cologne · Delhi
Melbourne · Amsterdam · Johannesburg · Auckland · Shenzhen

Lightning was

a race car.

He was shiny and fast.

He wanted one thing-

to win the big race!

Mater was a tow truck.

He was old and rusty.

He wanted one thing—

a best friend.

Mater lived
in a little town.
The streets were quiet.
All was calm.

One night,
Lightning got lost
on his way
to the big race.

He sped into
the little town.
Sheriff chased him.
Lightning got scared!

He flew into fences!

He crashed into cones!

He ripped up the road!

He made a big mess.

Lightning was
sent to jail.

He met Mater there.

Mater liked
Lightning right away.

Sally, the town lawyer,
and the other cars
wanted Lightning
to fix the road.

Lightning could not

leave town until

the job was done.

Lightning got to work.

He was unhappy.

Mater wanted

to show him some fun.

He took Lightning
tractor tipping.
It <u>was</u> fun.

Lightning told Mater
why he wanted
to win the big race.

He would have fame
and a new look.
He would be a winner!

Mater was happy.
He had a new best
friend.

Lightning fixed
the road at last!
The news reporters
found Lightning!

Mack the truck
was glad to see him!
It was time to go
to the big race.

Mater was sad
to see his buddy leave.
The other cars
were sad, too.

So Mater and his friends
went to the racetrack.
They helped Lightning.

But Lightning still
did not win.

He helped an old friend
finish the race instead.

Now he knew
that winning was not
what he wanted most.

What he wanted most
were friends.